No. 10. Serial. Price, 10 Cents.

THE

PULPIT AND ROSTRUM.

Sermons, Orations, Popular Lectures, &c.,

PHONOGRAPHICALLY REPORTED BY ANDREW J. GRAHAM AND CHAS. B. COLLAR

A TRIBUTE TO THE MEMORY OF

Washington Irving.

AN ADDRESS

BY

HON. EDWARD EVERETT,

BEFORE THE MASSACHUSETTS HISTORICAL SOCIETY. DELIVERED AT BOSTON, DECEMBER 15, 1859.

A SERMON

BY

REV. JOHN A. TODD,

DELIVERED AT TARRYTOWN, DEC. 11, 1859.

NEW YORK:
H. H. LLOYD & CO., 348 BROADWAY.
LONDON: Trubner & Co , 60 Paternoster Row.
SAN FRANCISCO: Warren & Carpenter, 167 Clay Street, General Agents for California.

January 15th, 1860.

THE DEATH OF WASHINGTON IRVING.

An Address by Hon. Edward Everett before the Massachusetts Historical Society. Delivered at Boston, Dec. 15, 1859.

I CORDIALLY concur in the resolutions which Mr. Longfellow has submitted to the Society. They do no more than justice to the merits and character of Mr. Irving, as a man and as a writer; and it is to me, sir, a very pleasing circumstance that a tribute like this to the Nestor of the prose writers of America—so just and so happily expressed—should be paid by the most distinguished of our American poets.

If the year 1769 is distinguished, above every other year of the last century, for the number of eminent men to which it gave birth, that of 1859 is thus far signalized in this century for the number of bright names which it has taken from us; and surely that of Washington Irving may be accounted with the brightest on the list.

It is eminently proper that we should take a respectful notice of his decease. He has stood for many years on the roll of our honorary members, and he has enriched the literature of the country with two first-class historical works, which, although from their subjects they possess a peculiar attraction for the people of the United States, are yet, in general interest, second to no cotemporary works in that department of literature. I allude, of course, to the "History of the Life and Voyages of Columbus" and the "Life of Washington."

Although Mr. Irving's devotion to literature as a profession—and a profession pursued with almost unequaled success—was caused by untoward events, which in ordinary cases would have proved the ruin of a life—a rare good fortune attended his literary career. Without having received a collegiate education, and destined first to the legal profession, which he abandoned as uncongenial, he had, in very early life, given promise of attaining a brilliant reputation as a writer. Some essays from his pen attracted notice before he reached his majority. A few years later, the numbers of the "Salmagundi," to which he was a principal contributor, enjoyed a success throughout the United States far beyond any former similar work, and not surpassed, if equaled, by anything which has since appeared.

This was followed by "Knickerbocker's History of New York," which at once placed Mr. Irving at the head of American humorists. In the class of compositions to which it belongs, I know of nothing happier than this work in our language. It has probably been read as widely, and with as keen a relish, as anything from Mr. Irving's pen. It would seem cynical to subject a work of this kind to an austere commentary, at least while we are paying a tribute to the memory of its lamented author. But I may be permitted to observe that, while this kind of writing fits well with the joyous temperament of youth, in the first flush of successful authorship, and is managed by Mr. Irving with great delicacy and skill, it is, in my opinion, better adapted for a *jeu d'esprit* in a magazine than for a work of considerable compass. To travesty an entire history seems to me a mistaken effort of ingenuity, and not well applied to the countrymen of William of Orange, Grotius, the De Witts, and Van Tromp.

This work first made Mr. Irving known in Europe. His friend, Mr. Henry Brevoort, one of the associate wits of the "Salmagundi," had sent a copy of it to Sir Walter Scott, himself chiefly known at that time as the most popular of the English poets of the day, though as such beginning to be outdone by the fresher brightness of Byron's inspiration. Scott, though necessarily ignorant of the piquant allusions to topics of cotemporary interest, and wholly destitute of sympathy with the spirit of the work, entered fully into its humor as a literary effort, and spoke of it with discrimination and warmth. His letter to Mr. Henry Brevoort is now in the possession of his son, our esteemed corresponding associate, Mr. J. Carson Brevoort, to whose liberality we are indebted for the curious panoramic drawing of the military works in the environs of Boston, executed by a British officer in 1775, which I have had the pleasure, on behalf of Mr. Brevoort, of tendering to the Society this evening. Mr. Carson Brevoort has caused a lithographic *fac-simile* of Sir Walter Scott's letter to be executed, and of this interesting relic he also offers a copy to the acceptance of the Society. The letter has been inserted in the very instructive article on Mr. Irving, in Allibone's invaluable dictionary of English and American authors; but as it is short, and may not be generally known to the Society, I will read it from the *fac-simile:*

MY DEAR SIR—I beg you to accept my best thanks for the uncommon degree of entertainment which I have received from the most excellently jocose history of New York. I am sensible that, as a stranger to American parties and politics, I must lose much of the concealed satire of the piece; but I must own that, looking at the simple and obvious meaning only, I have never read anything so closely resembling the style of Dean Swift as the annals of Diedrich Knickerbocker. I have been employed these few evenings in reading them aloud to Mrs. S., and two ladies who are our guests, and our sides have been absolutely sore with laughing. I think, too, there are passages which indicate that the author possesses powers of a different kind, and has some touches which remind me much of Sterne. I beg you will have the kindness to let me know when Mr. Irving takes pen in hand again, for assuredly I shall expect a very great treat, which I may chance never to hear of but through your kindness. Believe me, dear sir,

Your obliged humble servant, WALTER SCOTT.

ABBOTSFORD, 23*d April*, 1813.

After Mr. Irving had been led to take up his residence abroad, and to adopt literature as a profession and a livelihood—a resource to which he was driven by the failure of the commercial house of his relatives, of which he was nominally a partner—he produced in rapid succession a series of works which stood the test of English criticism, and attained a popularity not surpassed—hardly equaled—by that of any of his European cotemporaries. This fact, besides being attested by the critical journals of the day, may be safely inferred from the munificent prices paid by the great London bookseller, the elder Murray, for the copyright of several of his productions. He wrote, among other subjects, of English manners, sports, and traditions—national traits of character—certainly the most difficult topics for a foreigner to treat, and he wrote at a time when Scott was almost annually sending forth one of his marvelous novels; when the poetical reputation of Moore, Byron, Campbell, and Rogers was at the zenith; and the public appetite was consequently fed almost to satiety by these familiar domestic favorites. But notwithstanding these disadvantages and obstacles to success, he rose at once to a popularity of the most brilliant and enviable kind; and this, too, in a branch of literature which had not been cultivated with distinguished success in England since the time of Goldsmith, and, with the exception of Goldsmith, not since the days of Addison and Steele.

Mr. Irving's manner is often compared with Addison's, though, closely examined, there is no great resemblance between them, except that they both write in a simple, unaffected style, remote from the tiresome stateliness of Johnson and Gibbon. It was one of the witty, but rather ill-natured, sayings of Mr. Samuel Rogers, whose epigrams sometimes did as much injustice to his own kind and generous nature as they did to the victims of his pleasantry, that Washington Irving was Addison and water; a judgment which, if seriously dealt with, is altogether aside from the merits of the two writers, who have very little in common. Addison had received a finished classical education at the Charter House and at Oxford, was eminently a man of books, and had a decided taste for literary criticism. Mr. Irving, for a man of letters, was not a great reader, and if he possessed the critical faculty never exercised it. Addison quoted the Latin poets freely, and wrote correct Latin verses himself. Mr. Irving made no pretensions to a familiar acquaintance with the classics, and probably never made a hexameter in his life. Addison wrote some smooth English poetry, which Mr. Irving, I believe, never attempted; but, with the exception of two or three exquisite hymns (which will last as long as the English language does), one brilliant simile of six lines in the "Campaign," and one or two sententious but not very brilliant passages from Cato, not a line of Addison's poetry has been quoted for a hundred years. But Mr. Irving's peculiar vein of humor is not inferior in playful raciness to Addison's; his nicety of characterization is quite equal; his judgment upon all moral relations as sound and true; his human sympathies more comprehensive, tenderer, and chaster; and his poetical faculty, though never developed in verse, vastly above Addison's. One chord in the human heart, the pathetic, for whose sweet music Addison had no ear, Irving touched with the hand of a master. He learned that skill in the school of early disappointment.

In this respect the writer was in both cases reflected in the man. Addison, after a protracted suit, made an "ambitious match" with a termagant peeress; Irving, who would as soon have married Hecate as a woman like the Countess of Warwick, buried a blighted hope, never to be rekindled, in the grave of a youthful sorrow.

As miscellaneous essayists, in which capacity only they can be compared, Irving exceeds Addison in versatility and range, quite as much as Addison exceeds Irving in the far less important quality of classical tincture; while, as a great national historian, our countryman reaped laurels in a field which Addison never entered.

Mr. Irving's first great historical work, "The Life and Voyages of Columbus," appeared at London and New York in 1828. Being at Bordeaux in the winter of 1825–6, he received a letter from Mr. Alexander H. Everett, then minister of the United States in Spain, informing him that a work was passing through the press, containing a collection of documents relative to the voyages of Columbus, among which were many of a highly important nature recently discovered in the public archives. This was the now well-known work of Navarette, the Secretary of the Royal Spanish Academy of History. Mr. Everett, in making this communication to Mr. Irving, suggested that the translation of Navarette's volumes into English, by some American scholar, would be very desirable; Mr. Irving concurred in this opinion, and having previously intended to visit Madrid, shortly afterward repaired to that capital, with a view to undertake the proposed translation.

Navarette's collection was published soon after Mr. Irving's arrival at Madrid, and finding it rich in original documents hitherto unknown, which threw additional light on the discovery of America, he conceived the happy idea (instead of a simple translation) of preparing from them and other materials liberally placed at his disposal, in the public and private libraries of Spain (and especially that of Mr. Obadiah Rich, our consul at Valencia, with whom Mr. Irving was domesticated at Madrid, and who possessed a collection of manuscripts and books of extreme value), a new history of the greatest event of modern times, drawn up in the form of a life of Columbus. He addressed himself with zeal and assiduity to the execution of this happy conception, and in about two years the work, in four octavo volumes, was ready for the press. When it is considered that much of the material was to be drawn from ancient manuscripts and black-letter chronicles in a foreign tongue, it is a noble monument of the industry, as well as the literary talent, of its author.

That these newly discovered materials for a life of Columbus, and a history of the great discovery, should have fallen directly into the hands of an American writer, so well qualified to make a good use of them as Mr. Irving, and that the credit of producing the first adequate memorial of this all-important event should have been thus secured to the United States by their most popular author, is certainly a very pleasing coincidence.

The limits of this occasion require me to pass over two or three popular works of a light cast, for which Mr. Irving collected the materials while carrying on his historical researches in Spain, as also those which issued from his industrious and fertile pen, after his return to the United States in 1832. At this period of his life he began seriously to contemplate the preparation of his last great production—the "Life of Washington." This subject had been pressed upon him, while he was yet in Europe, by Mr. Archibald Constable, the celebrated publisher at Edinburgh, and Mr. Irving determined to undertake it as soon as his return to America should bring him within reach of the necessary documents. Various circumstances occurred to prevent the execution of the project at this time, especially his appointment as minister to Spain, and his residence in that country from 1842 to 1846. On his return to America, at the close of his mission, he appears to have applied himself diligently to the long-meditated undertaking, though he proceeded but slowly, at first, in its execution. The first volume appeared in 1855, and the four following in rapid succession. The work was finally completed the present year—at the close of the life of its illustrious author, and of a literary career of such rare brilliancy and success.

It would be altogether a work of supererogation to engage in any general commentary on the merits of Mr. Irving's two great historical works, and the occasion is not appropriate for a critical analysis of them. They have taken a recognized place in the historical literature of the age, and stand, by all confession, in the front rank of those works of history of which this century, and especially this country, has been so honorably prolific. Reserving a distinguished place apart for the venerable name of Marshall, Mr. Irving leads the long line of American historians—first in time and not second in beauty of style, conscientious accuracy, and skillful arrangement of materials. As his two works treat respectively of themes, which for purely American interest stand at the head of all single subjects of historical research, so there is no one of our writers to whom the united voice of the country would with such cheerful unanimity have intrusted their composition.

From the time he entered for life upon a literary career, Mr. Irving gave himself almost exclusively to its pursuits. He filled the office of *chargé d'affaires* for a short time in London, prior to his return to the United States, and that of minister to Spain from 1842 to 1846. His diplomatic dispatches in that capacity are among the richest of the treasures which lie buried in the public archives at Washington.

A more beautiful life than Mr. Irving's can hardly be imagined. Not uncheckered with adversity, his early trials, under the soothing influence of time, without subduing the natural cheerfulness of his disposition, threw over it a mellow tenderness, which breathes in his habitual trains of thought, and is reflected in the amenity of his style. His misfortunes in business, kindly overruled by a gracious Providence, laid the foundation of literary success, reputation, and prosperity. At two different periods of his career he engaged in public life; entering without ambition; performing its duties with diligence and punctuality; and leaving it without regret. He was appointed *chargé d'affaires* to London under Gen. Jackson's administration, and minister to Spain under Mr. Tyler's, the only instances perhaps in this century in which a distinguished executive appointment has been made without a thought as to the political opinions of the person appointed. Mr. Irving's appointment to Spain was made on the recommendation of Mr. Webster, who told me that he regarded it as one of the most honorable memorials of his administration of the Department of State. It was, no doubt, a pleasing circumstance to Mr. Irving to return in his advancing years, crowned with public honors, to the country where, in earlier life, he had pursued his historical studies with so much success; but public life had no attractions for him. The respect and affection of the community followed him to his retirement; he lived in prosperity without an ill-wisher; finished the work which was given him to do, amid the blessings of his countrymen, and died amid loving kindred in honor and peace.

THE DEATH OF WASHINGTON IRVING.

A Discourse delivered in the Second Reformed Dutch Church of Tarrytown, New York, on Sabbath Morning, December 11, 1859, *by the Pastor, Rev. John A. Todd.*

"For behold the Lord, the Lord of Hosts, doth take away from Jerusalem and from Judah the stay and the staff, the whole stay of bread, and the whole stay of water; the mighty man, and the man of war, the judge, and the prophet, and the prudent, and the ancient; the captain of fifty and the honorable man, and the counselor, and the cunning artificer, and the eloquent orator."—Isaiah iii. 1–3.

The subject of this chapter is continued from the one which precedes it. The threatenings of God against Judah are here set forth in solemn and impressive array. The opening portion of the chapter is occupied with the general announcement that the people were about to be deprived of the supports upon which they principally depended, and among these are mentioned, as the chief and most important, "the whole stay of bread, and the whole stay of water," the food and the drink which were essential to the preservation of life. Immediately following, we have a list of the public men—eminent and conspicuous for their official position, and for their natural endowments and genius—who were about to be removed from the nation, and among them we find the military, the civil, and the religious functionaries of the land.

At the next step in the progress of national decline, and as, indeed, the necessary consequence of what had just taken place, the affairs of the state are intrusted to the guidance of weak and unskillful hands. Insurrection against the established order of society, mutual violence and aggression, and wide-spread anarchy are the fruits of a government whose power is not guided by the dictates of wisdom and justice. And, at length, no one being found willing to accept of public office—a singular condition of society, to which in this country we have never yet attained—the strong oppress the weak; the authority of law, the guaranty of personal rights, the security of life and property are subverted and swept away, and the national existence is numbered among the things that were. In all this, the prophet desired those whom he addressed to recognize the hand of God—that God who "doeth according to His will in the army of heaven, and among the inhabitants of the earth." He did not allow their thoughts to rest upon the Chaldeans, as the primary cause of the events which he predicted, when in fact they were only the *instruments* employed by a superior and all-controlling Power. But he led their contemplations away upward and onward, along the narrow channel through which the Divine energy had rolled forward to its effect until they found themselves in the presence of the Lord Jehovah himself, the everlasting God who fainteth not, neither is weary; and saw in Him the great and sovereign disposer of national, as well as of individual destinies, who raises up one and casts down another according to His righteous will.

In the last verse of the preceding chapter, the prophet had called upon the people "to cease from man whose breath is in his nostrils"—that is, to cease from reposing their trust in any human protection, and from regarding with a confidence which shut out God from the government of His own universe, the high endowments of created mind. And in the text, he presents the argument by which he sought to convince their understandings, and to persuade their hearts into compliance with his exhortation. That argument lay in the fact that God was about to deprive them of the various means of support and protection upon which they so inconsiderately relied—the food upon which they subsisted, and the men of illustrious station and pre-eminent intellect who constituted, in their estimation, the bulwark and glory of their land.

"For, behold," says he, "the Lord, as the sovereign disposer, even Jehovah of Hosts, the self-existent and eternal one, is about to take away from Jerusalem and Judah, not only from the capital, but from the whole kingdom, the stay and the staff, all kinds of support, and, first of all, the whole stay of bread, and the whole stay of water, the supply of their physical and necessary wants. And next in the catalogue of supports and resources of which God was about to deprive them, the great men of the commonwealth, thus—as the rendering may be literally given*—"Hero and warrior, judge and prophet, divine and elder, the chief of fifty, and the favorite, and the counselor and the ingenious artificer, and the man who is skillful of speech"—that is, possessed of genius to mold and fashion language, and to clothe the creations of the mind in the attractive forms of persuasion, of melody, and of beauty.

Such is the meaning of the text. And thus did the prophet teach the Jewish people of old, that there was a Power above all human power, upon which they were dependent, and in which they ought to put their trust—that man, whatever may be his prowess in battle, or his wisdom in counsel; whatever may be the insinuating and resistless enchantment of his genius, whether revealed in thoughts bodied forth, and transferred by the cunning artifice of letters to the written page, or breathed by the living voice in tones of eloquence and power upon the listening ear—is, after all, but a *creature*, whose breath is in his nostrils, whose heart is exposed and vulnerable to the shafts of death, and who, before the next moment has winged

---

* Chiefly, but not entirely, as given by Prof. Alexander, on Isaiah, *in loco*.

its way into eternity, may be torn from those who delight in his beautiful and multiplied creations, or who rely for safety upon his aid.

You have no doubt, my hearers, already apprehended the object of these remarks. Your thoughts have outstripped the words that were designed to awaken and direct them, and have gathered in solemn silence around that event which has cast a shadow of gloom upon this whole nation, and especially upon the community in which we live. Not that the idea of Death is unfamiliar to our minds; not that he does not often come into this, and into every community, wherever the sons and daughters of Adam have carried the frail clay of humanity; but because, in this instance, his stroke has fallen upon a distinguished victim, and he has removed from among us the presence of one toward whom our hearts went forth in unwonted admiration and regard. Every day, either here or elsewhere, and often in many places at one and the same moment, is Death exerting his solemn power upon the race of man. In the humble cottage on some mountain slope, in some shaded valley or distant forest, or in the living wilderness of some great city, are the young and the old, the brave and the fair, passing away in unbroken procession to the dust of the sepulcher, and to the destinies of the life to come. But the great world without does not regard it. Like the leaves of autumn that strew our pathway, they sink into the grave, and their death is crowded from recollection by the never-ending succession of new events. But when the tall and graceful trees of the forest—the monarchs whose heads towered above the general attitude—are brought down by some resistless blow, their fall is attended with a louder crash, and the earth itself trembles beneath the shock. So, when the men who walk upon the loftier heights of place and power—when those whose intellectual stature as they move along the paths of science, of history, of literature, and of art, renders them pre-eminent above the general mass, are laid prostrate by the stroke of Death, the event impresses itself more vividly upon the minds of men, and calls out from its hidden springs in the heart a profounder sentiment of sorrow.

I know not what may be done or spoken elsewhere in regard to the departure out of this life of that illustrious, and honored, and beloved citizen, whom we, in this community, were so proud to call our friend and neighbor, but whatever it may be, I can not bring myself to believe that you, my hearers, are willing that he should pass away from among us never more to return, and that his dust should be laid down to mingle with that of parents and dearest kindred, by the shadow of that old Dutch Church, which is the mother of us all, without some recognition of his individuality—some words of tender feeling, of heart-felt sorrow, some expression of love and reverence for his memory, some offering of praise and thanksgiving to God for the excellent gifts, both of head and heart, with which He was pleased to endow him, and some attempt to gather up and to bring home, for our nobler and more spiritual uses, the solemn lessons of the dispensation which took him from us. His is a name to be revered and cherished. His story shines upon our country's annals. And now that he has gone from us, and from the land he loved so well, he has bequeathed to us in his unblemished life, in his recorded words, and in his illustrious name, an inheritance worthy to be highly prized, to be sacredly guarded. A country's glory is the collected glory of the great men whom God has given her—their high achievements, their noble spirits, their memorable names. And it is right that they should have their monuments not merely in the mute and icy marble that marks the spot where their ashes rest, but in the warm, the living, throbbing hearts of all her sons.

——"Think not such names
Are common sounds; they have a music in them,
An odorous recollection; they are a part
Of the old glorious past. Their country knows

And loves the lofty echo which gives back
The memory of the buried great,
And calls to valor and to victory,
To goodness and to freedom."

When such a man dies—when his name is stricken from the roll of living men, and given in sacred charge to the historic muse, that she may "march with it down to the latest times," it is not meet that his honored dust should be put away out of sight in darkness and in silence without some tribute to his character, to his life, and to his fame. For when we thus give our offerings of love and admiration to that which God made so fair, and yet so wonderful in capacity and power, we praise God in His works, we glorify His matchless and infinite skill, and we do honor to the dignity of that nature which is able so to appreciate and so to delight in the higher exhibitions of the wisdom and goodness of our Creator.

It is a solemn event when God comes by His providence, and removes from the midst of a nation the mind which He has most highly endowed. Insensible must be that heart, and deaf to the voice of instruction must be that spirit, that does not receive with reverent humility, with docile submission, the impressive lessons which such an event is adapted and designed to teach.

It is a sad thing to utter. It is almost startling, to us who have been accustomed so long to look upon him as he has moved in quiet and unobtrusive dignity among us, but the hand of God has transferred the thought from the records of possibility to those of actual fact. Washington Irving, the patriarch of American literature—the acomplished scholar—the admirable historian—the elegant writer—the wonderful magician, who evoked from the realms of thought the spirit of romance and beauty, and breathed it upon every hill and valley, upon every shady retreat, and every wandering brook that hastens on to join this noble river that pours its majestic volume into the sea; aye, and upon the very air that fans the summer verdure, or whistles through the branches of the wintry wood around us—the pure patriot—the diplomatist, watchful for his country's honor, and yet skillful in the arts of preserving peace—the kind and beloved neighbor—the faithful friend, and, what is better than all, because it constituted him the "highest style of man," the modest and benevolent Christian, the sincere believer and disciple of the Lord Jesus Christ—Washington Irving is dead. Dead, did I say? No! He has just begun to live. His spirit has gone up to the enjoyment of a higher sphere, and its power upon the kindred spirit of his race has been consecrated by the solemn mystery of its departure. God has given to him the precious boon of a two-fold life—the life eternal of the glorified in heaven, and the life of an undying memory in the hearts of men. And can we say of such a one that he is dead? True, he has gone from us, and on earth we shall see his face no more.

> "But strew his ashes to the wind,
> Whose sword or voice has served mankind—
> And is he dead whose glorious mind
> Lifts thine on high?
> To live in hearts we leave behind
> Is not to die."

We have lost his welcome presence, and it is for that we mourn. But his grave is with us, and here it will remain for generations to come, the shrine of unnumbered pilgrim feet. From the lofty eminence upon which he stood, conspicuous to the eyes of the world, from his position of intellectual greatness and spotless dignity, he has passed away. The sepulcher has claimed all of him that was mortal for its own. His eye is quenched; his arm is palsied; the tongue that was ever eloquent with the words of kindness is hushed to the ears of living men forever; the pen that distilled upon the written page the subtile creations of his brain, the ideal forms all fresh and fair from the realms of intellectual beauty, in which his spirit loved to linger, lies where he left it, dead and silent, like the clay from which the living soul has departed. And on this Sabbath morning, while we are gathered in the house of God, his honored remains are sleeping by the side of her whom he called by the holy name of "Mother," who loved him while living, and whose memory he loved when dying, in the grave which he had appointed for his last repose. There—there may they sleep in peace, until these heavens be no more, and in the last day be raised again to the glorious resurrection of the just!

It is not my purpose, nor is this the proper time, to trace the career or to pronounce the eulogy of the illustrious dead. Born in the city of New York, at No. 131 William Street, about midway between John and Fulton streets, and only a few steps from the old North Dutch Church, on the 3d of April, 1783, and dying in his own quiet home on the banks of the Hudson, on the 28th of November, 1859, he attained to the ripe old age of 76 years 7 months and 25 days. And then he received the fulfillment of the promise: "Thou shalt come to thy grave in a full age, like as a shock of corn cometh in his season."

The record of his life, from the home of his childhood, upward and onward along the path of toil and triumph which he trod, with quiet courage and ascending step, until he reached the last and loftiest height of his earthly being, from which he went still forward and upward, "with his old stride from glory to glory," has been carried on the wings of fame to the farthest hamlet of our country, and to the remotest corners of the civilized world.

It is enough to say that, beginning his literary career at the age of nineteen, and sending forth the first of his principal works at the age of twenty-six, his progress to the end was but the continual repetition of success. Of him it may be said, what was said of another, that,

"He kept Victory on the run,
Till Fame was out of breath."

The last work, and perhaps the greatest, that he ever wrote, the "Life of Washington," he completed but a few months before his death. In that his labors came to a close—the star of his genius culminated to its zenith; and while the vestal fire of patriotism shall burn in the national heart, and while the English language—the grandest of living tongues—shall express the thoughts of living men, that work shall perpetuate the names of George Washington and Washington Irving, canonized in the fellowship of glory—the Father of his Country and the Father of his Country's Literature. The triumphs of his splendid morning were surpassed by those which he achieved beneath the mellow radiance of his setting sun; and thus, by the labors of his declining years, he appropriated to himself a share in the sentiment which, it has been affirmed, could be applied to none but Milton—that "he was the only man who ever eclipsed his own fame by a higher and brighter noon; who, after winning an immortality for his youth, gave it back to oblivion by the achievements of his age."

But his character wore another aspect; he was something more than the man of genius. Honored as he was, the world over, he was yet loved as well, and as much, as he was honored. No one could mingle in his society, though the opportunity were but brief, without feeling the magnetic influence of his nature. In his countenance, as well as in the placid flow of his language, and in the sentiments which he habitually entertained, the one feature which distinguished his character as a man, and stood out in pleasant and winning prominence, expressed itself to all who knew him in the single word—peace. For the struggles of intellectual warfare, the sharp excitement of opposing convictions, it is almost needless to say that he had no taste. In the atmosphere of mutual love, in the fragrance of gentle sympathies, he found his congenial element, and there he was ever at home. On more than one occasion, when he debated questions of ecclesiastical order, and subjects of a kindred nature have engaged the conversation of friends in his hearing, he has been known to interpose with the remark: "Let us live in love. We are all striving for the same object, and going to the same place of rest; and why should there be contentions by the way?" His mild expostulation at once silenced the discord of controversy, and brought back the reign of peace.

Attached he undoubtedly was to the polity and form of worship of the particular denomination of Christians to which he belonged, but his heart was too large, his sympathies too noble, not to recognize and appreciate, with profound respect, the excellence and labors of other denominations that maintained the vital principles of Christianity. No one could fairly apply to him the lines which Goldsmith so unfairly applied to Burke:

> "Who, born for the universe, narrowed his mind,
> And to party gave up what was meant for mankind."

He had a broad and catholic spirit, which he manifested not only in words, but also in deeds. The pecuniary means which he subscribed and paid to promote the general interests and efficiency of the Reformed Dutch Church in this village, together with other contributions to religious and benevolent purposes, indicate very clearly the liberal sentiments which occupied his mind and heart—sentiments which are the never-failing result of true piety in union with intellectual greatness. One of the last acts of his life—occurring in November, the very month in which he died—was to present to the library of the Western Theological Seminary of the Old-School Presbyterian Church, at Alleghany City, Pennsylvania, through the hands of a venerable and valued friend residing in Pittsburgh, a beautiful copy of his "Life of Washington." I had myself the pleasure of examining the volumes a few days before they were sent to their destination, and was struck, on reading the brief lines of presentation which he had written on a blank leaf of the first volume, by the traces of that graceful modesty which ever distinguished him, and by the simple affection which he cherished for his friend. We can not wonder, when we contemplate his life, that his death awakened in so many hearts the sad sense of personal affliction, or that so many unfeigned mourners were found in the slow procession which followed his remains to the tomb.

In quiet simplicity—in all the gentleness of sunny and genial childhood—with a heart overflowing with kindness and good-will toward all men, and filled with submissive and grateful humility before God—with a spirit mild and amiable by nature, and rendered still more lovely by the ennobling influence of the religion of Jesus Christ—which he firmly believed and consistently professed, he passed his days among us until they closed with the closing year, amid peaceful scenes, and under gentle skies, which were in singular and beautiful harmony with the spirit that ruled his life. In him, if ever, did the blended lineaments of greatness and humility illustrate the fair ideal upon whose living realization the Martyr-Student of Cambridge so earnestly longed to look!

> —— "Oh, I would walk
> A weary journey to the farthest verge
> Of the big world to kiss that good man's hand,
> Who in the blaze of wisdom and of art
> Preserves a lowly mind; and to his God,
> Feeling the sense of his own littleness,
> Is as a child in meek simplicity!"

Conscious that the powers of his physical frame were giving way—that "the silver cord was about to be loosed," and "the pitcher to be broken at the fountain"—he anticipated his departure at no distant day. But a short time before his death, while assisting to convey to the tomb the remains of an aged and venerable friend, he was heard to remark that the service which he was then performing for another, he would soon need for himself.

On another occasion, during the month of November, as he was taking leave of one who has often worshiped with us in the sanctuary—a clergyman of the Presbyterian Church, no less revered for his character than for his labors and his years, to whom he was greatly attached, and who was about to return to his Western home, from which he had come to spend the summer on the banks of the Hudson—he referred with touching emotions to their declining age, and to the probability that this would be their final parting. But, he immediately added, although they might never meet again on earth, there was a better land, and they would temper their present sorrow with the hope of a reunion in the life to come. God grant that when his surviving friend shall follow him thither, that hope may have a full and glorious realization. But perhaps the most solemn and tender expression of his anticipations in regard to death was that which was among the last, if it was not, indeed, the very last, that he was known to utter. Only five days before he closed his eyes forever upon the light of earth, he stood by his mother's grave—that mother whose memory was ever so dear—and pointing to the spot by the side of it, which he had selected for his own, he said calmly to the friend at his side, "I shall be soon there."

Dear old man! he has reached the goal of his earthly journey. His prophecy is fulfilled. Crowned with the wreath of immortal fame, loaded with the benedictions of loving hearts, full of years, full of peace, he has gone to his rest. There his head shall recline upon its lowly pillow, and his Redeemer shall guard his sacred dust.

It is delightful to think that the same benignant Providence which smiled upon his life, gave to the time of his death and burial the placid beauty of unclouded skies, the brightness of warm and golden sunshine, the glory of autumnal hills bathed in its effulgence, and rendered pure and sweet by the gentle winds that blow upon them from the majestic river that rolls beneath. It is more delightful to think of the love and veneration that swelled the hearts of the congregated thousands that came from near and far to pay their homage to his genius and his worth. But it is most delightful of all to think that the patriarch's work was done, and that he was waiting for the call of that blessed Master whose love transforms the gates of death into the gates of glory to the soul. Yes—yes. It is true, my friends, we have nothing to regret, nothing to mourn, but our own loss, our own bereavement.

> "Nothing is here for tears, nothing to wail
> Or knock the breast, no weakness, no contempt,
> Dispraise or blame, nothing but well and fair,
> And what may quiet us in a death so noble."

And now, beloved hearers, what is the lesson which we are to learn from this solemn dispensation? Is not God teaching us individually and as a nation that every earthly stay and staff is but frail and uncertain at best? Does He not remind us, when the great men of our country come down from their high places to sleep in the dust, that all that pertains to time is imperfect, transient, perishing? One by one the great lights of a nation are extinguished by death. The men of brave hearts and giant intellects—warriors, statesmen, historians, poets, philosophers, divines—they pass away, and who shall take their vacant places? Who shall fight the battles, stand at the helm of government, record the march of history, sing the song of joy, chant the dirge of sorrow, explore the mysteries of science, defend the cause of truth and righteousness, and plead with men in the accents of persuasion, and with God in the accents of prayer? Ah! my hearers, we know full well that none but God can give the arms of strength, and the hearts of courage, and the intellects of power. God, *and* God *only, is great.* Let us, therefore, take refuge in Him. With love for His character, with trust in His promises, with confidence in His goodness, with obedience to His will, let us go to Him, and pray that our fellow-men, that our whole country may go with us, and then "the place of her defense shall be the munitions of rocks," and "upon her assemblies God will create a cloud and smoke by day, and the shining of a flaming fire by night." "In His name shall they rejoice, and in His righteousness shall they be exalted. He shall be the glory of our strength. For the Lord himself shall be our defense, and the Holy One of Israel shall be our King."

Let me entreat you also, beloved friends, to be admonished by the providence of God, that, to every one here assembled, life is short and death is certain. Rank, wealth, learning, genius—they are all nothing to the stern regard of Death. With promiscuous blow, and without respect to persons, the high and the low, the small and the great, are laid prostrate together at His feet. The experience of the past, the events of every departing day, the lessons of that startling providence whose echoes are yet lingering in our ears, all combine to impress the great conviction upon our hearts: "All flesh is grass; and the glory of man as the flower of the field. His breath goeth forth, he returneth to his earth; in that very day his thoughts perish. God hath spoken once; twice have I heard this, that power belongeth unto God." True, indeed, it is, that death, as in the example before us, is the natural and fitting termination of a life protracted beyond three-score years and ten. True, also, it undoubtedly is, that the sentiment expressed by the ill-starred son of genius, whose dust lies sleeping on the banks of the pastoral Nith—

> "Oh, Death! the poor man's dearest friend,
> The kindest and the best!"

has met with many a sad response from the children of poverty and sorrow. Death does sometimes come in the vesture of friendship and gladness, and smile upon the suffering, the heart-broken, and the weary. He does sometimes come to the child of God, waiting and anxious for the final hour when he may depart and be with Christ, which is far better, with a message like that which broke from an angel's lips upon the startled air of Bethlehem, "Fear not, for behold I bring you good tidings of great joy!" But, believe me, oftener far does he come to men in stern and appalling aspect. And thus, my hearers, unless he be disarmed of his terrors by your individual and personal reliance upon the blood of Christ for safety, will Death inevitably come to you. The accumulations of laborious years, the gratification of the body and the mind by the two-fold ministry of nature and of art, the bonds of love, the tender associations, the maturity of age, the strength of manhood, the buoyancy of youth—what are they all to Death? He tears men away from wealth and power, from pomp and pleasure. When the bud of enterprise is unfolding itself into the flower of success; when hope stands with sparkling eye to greet the approaching fulfillment; when victory, like an eagle comes sailing down the heavens to perch upon the standard that has been upborne with heroic courage through a long and weary struggle; when the cup of joy is mantling to the brim, and the heart is bounding with exultation; then, then—suddenly—there is a flash, like the bolt from heaven, and the noon-tide brightness is changed into the midnight gloom. The man is dead. His heart is still. His eye is dark. His hands are folded across his icy breast. They carry him out, and they lay him down in his grave. Oh, how true are those words which burst from the agonized heart of Edmund Burke, when he contemplated the death of his only son, "What shadows we are, and what shadows we pursue!"

My dear friends, there is no escape for us. We must all die. But in the glorious gospel of Jesus Christ there is an antidote against the power of Death. With Him is the fountain of life, and His people shall drink from it forever. The body may sink, but the spirit shall rise. The clay may crumble; but the soul shall mount in glory. "I am the resurrection and the life," saith the Christ; "he that believeth in Me, though he were dead, yet shall he live. And whosoever liveth and believeth in Me shall never die." The garland of immortality that withered in Eden shall bloom again for the righteous in the paradise of God.

To-day, then, with the admonition of Providence sounding in your ears, with the vision of a new-made grave before you, let me come to you, in the name of Christ, with the offer of everlasting life. He gives freely—He gives abundantly. Oh! love Him, trust Him, follow Him. Then, when the spirit is about to depart from the falling tabernacle of the body, it may pour itself into that triumphant shout of God's redeemed, "O death, where is thy sting? O grave, where is thy victory?" The sting of death is sin, and the strength of sin is the law. But thanks be to God, which giveth us the victory through our Lord Jesus Christ.

LIST OF THE WORKS

OF

WASHINGTON IRVING, BAYARD TAYLOR, and others.

PUBLISHED FOR THE AUTHORS,

BY

G. P. PUTNAM, NEW YORK.

Terms: Cash in New York.

Any Book in the list will be delivered in any part of the United States, free of expense or postage, on receipt of the money.

*** The Life of Washington being now complete, the Publisher is prepared to furnish sets of all the works of Mr. Irving, uniformly bound, in 21 vols., in various styles, as in the following list.

The whole have been revised, and the present editions are well printed on good paper. Each volume has one or more steel plates or vignettes.

IRVING'S WHOLE WORKS—SUNNYSIDE EDITION (Including Washington) On tinted paper, with Steel Vignettes; neatly put up in boxes. Complete in 21 vols, 12mo, cloth, $28; half calf extra, or antique, $47. For other styles see catalogue.

IRVING'S WORKS—SUNNYSIDE EDITION. (Omitting Washington.) Same style as above, in boxes. Complete in 16 vols., with vignettes, cloth, $20; other styles from $22 to $50. See catalogue.

IRVING'S LIFE OF WASHINGTON—1. THE POPULAR EDITION IN 12mo. Complete in 5 vols., 12mo, cloth, $7; sheep, $8.50. 2. THE SUNNYSIDE EDITION IN 12mo. On tinted paper, with 24 Steel Plates and 24 Wood Cuts. Complete in 5 vols., 12mo, cloth, $8; half calf extra, or antique, $13. 3. THE LIBRARY EDITION, LARGE TYPE.—Complete in 5 vols., 8vo, with Maps, &c., cloth, $10; sheep, $12.50; half calf, $16. 4. THE MOUNT VERNON EDITION.—5 vols. 8vo, (like the last), with all the Illustrations on Wood and Steel, half mor. gilt edges, $22; the same, full calf extra, $25. 5. THE ILLUSTRATED EDITION.—(With 102 Engravings on Steel, and numerous Wood Cuts.) 5 vols., imperial 8vo, large paper, cloth, $20; half calf, or mor., extra, $30; full mor., extra, $36. THE 5TH AND OTHER SEPARATE VOLS. OF "WASHINGTON," TO COMPLETE SETS.—For the present any Vol. will be supplied to match the original binding in cloth. Subscribers should complete their sets at once

IRVING'S WORKS—Separate Vols, in 12mo. KNICKERBOCKER'S NEW YORK; cloth, $1 25. SKETCH BOOK; cloth, $1 25. COLUMBUS, 3 vols; cloth, $4 00. BRACEBRIDGE HALL; cloth, $1 25. TALES OF A TRAVELLER; cloth, $1 25. ASTORIA; cloth, $1 50. CRAYON MISCELLANY; cloth, $1 25. CAPT. BONNEVILLE; cloth, $1 25. OLIVER GOLDSMITH: cloth $1 25. MAHOMET, 2 vols; cloth, $2 50. GRENADA: cloth, $1 25. ALHAMBRA; cloth, $1 25. WOLFERT'S ROOST; cloth, $1 25.

www.ingramcontent.com/pod-product-compliance
Lightning Source LLC
LaVergne TN
LVHW011138110826
845150LV00008B/2386
* 9 7 8 1 4 1 8 1 9 3 1 2 6 *